THE DOG KUBLA
DREAMS MY LIFE

To Mary
Thanks for all
your Kindness
Warm Regards

Anne

Galway, March
1994

The publishers gratefully acknowledge the support of

The Arts Council/An Chomhairle Ealaíon.

ANNE KENNEDY

THE DOG KUBLA DREAMS MY LIFE

WITH DRAWINGS BY ALLISON JUDD

SALMON  POETRY

First published in 1994 by
Salmon Publishing Limited,
A division of Poolbeg Enterprises Ltd,
123 Baldoyle Industrial Estate
Baldoyle, Dublin 13, Ireland.

A catalogue record for this book is available from the British Library.

ISBN 1 897648 12 X

Front Cover Photography by Gillian Buckley
Illustrations by Allison Judd
Back Cover Photograph by Yann Studios
Cover design by Poolbeg Group Services Ltd.
Set by Mac Book Limited in Palatino
Printed by The Guernsey Press Limited,
Vale, Guernsey, Channel Islands.

To My Children
Allison, Catherine, Stephanie,
Maura and Miles

Acknowledgements are due to the following:

Geraldine Daly for her generous technical assistance

RTE Radio 1: *Sunday Miscellany,*
Scenes from a Return Journey, Just a Thought,
where some of the poems were broadcast.

Publications where some of the poems first
appeared: *The Salmon, Poetry Ireland Review,*
Fortnight, Criterion, Writing in the West, Southern
Humanities Review, Free Lunch, Women's Work, Living
Landscape, The Great Book of Ireland,
The Honest Ulsterman.

Special thanks to Ron Offen of *Free Lunch*
for his critical insight.

Contents

Out There

California

Gramercy Place, 1939

Against the white stucco wall
a small girl
with curls
in an organdy dress.
Her hand rests
in another's
large, dark and strong.
The black face shines,
shattered with lines,
where fine spray
scatters from the hose
and paints halos
round the roses,
where all their shadows fall
against the white stucco wall.

Rendezvous: Los Angeles, 1944

'All the forgiving couples hurry on to
dinner and their nights...'

Robert Lowell

No shadows, summer noon,
out of the Moorish doorway comes
an hourglass woman
rice powdered
raven haired.
The building's pleated minaret
curdles in fruitless orange light.

She checks her seams
sniffs slyly
for tell-tale scent of lover
looks right, looks left
hurries off
her heels tick tocking
down the empty street.

Her lucite bag
sticks to her bare knee,
glued shells and feathers
tacky in the heat.

Her lover won't emerge
from satin sheets
before dusk stubbles the palm trees.

Two-tone tasselled loafers
nautical jacket
4 - F
'flat feet'.

Later, behind chintz crossovers
she serves a casserole,
assuring her tired husband
her day's been boring too,
while beneath the dinette light
her ankle bracelet gleams.

Hearts and Flowers

Mary June's mother is soaking a heart.
She's steeped it for days in cornmeal,
while out in the garden their turtle
licks flies.

Mary June's mother loves sailors,
young ones
young sailors in tight white bell bottoms
slick curls escaping from their
dishy caps.

Mary June's mother likes kissing sailors.
She kisses them and she cries
when the Andrews Sisters sing
Don't sit under the appletree
with anyone else but me
and she drinks whiskey
while the heart lies macerating
in its own juice.

Mary June and me
we sit among the dusty
ivy and wait
for the turtle's rough tongue
to dart after insects
while the steaming heart softens.

When Fred comes home from work
he doubts his wife knows how to cook
the heart,
especially since she's drunk
and singing.

We all sit down too early for dinner
and watch the chambered heart
carved up.
If we don't eat
there'll be a scene,
the food flung out
or scraped into the dog's dish.

That night she has a party
for the sailors;
Jasmine is blooming in the garden
and cars zoom past
just beyond the wall.
Her pompadour is shining
and Fred keeps losing track of his wife.
We know she's locked in the bathroom
on the floor with a sailor.

Outside
in the jasmine-scented night
the turtle moves with reptilian sureness,
his flippers stirring
scattered scraps of heart.

Early Times

Under an umbrella of Brazilian Pepper
my mother drinks and dreams
draws deep on her Phillip Morris
floats smoke rings above her head
while clouds of insects
halo a citronella candle.

Wax drips down rippled glass,
withered olives drop
pocking the pavement
around her patio chair.

My urgent questions
drift off with the smoke,
ice laughs in her glass.
She stirs her bourbon
Early Times
her drink.

I grab the candle
to smell the lemon deeper.
The pads of my fingers burn
against the boiling glass.
Painprints code my panic –

My hand in a glass of cold water
I listen for the click, click, click
of fresh ice
Early Times
after midnight.

Gravity

Alice
you knelt in the dunes all summer
with your silver trowel,
planting marram grass and succulents.
When the Santa Anas scoured the dunes
shaking the loft where we slept late,
we would find you in morning fog
kneeling again,
replanting your smothered garden.

Your husband Hans
spent your fortune on drink
and pretty nurses.
Defunct brain surgeon,
he ripped conversation out by the roots
and throttled thought;
shouting that gravity worked in reverse,
insisting we were all straining
to fly off the earth,
not to stay anchored to it.
A hiccup in the planets' spin
and we would soon swim
in streams of circling dust.
Everything:
trowels, dunes, Alice, Hans, daughters
all of Oxnard, and myself,
the watchful guest.

All that summer I lay
on the burning beach
reading Robinson Jeffers'
The Women At Point Sur,
and wondering what thrilling force
drove these women out in gales
to embrace one another;
while behind me
just out of sight,
that force was pouring earthwards
from your silver trowel.

It linked us to the fog,
the wind, the dunes,
the shuddering nights and sly surf,
and to you, Hans,
pontificating on the stars.

Those days in the dunes exist now
only in bands of dust
orbiting endlessly with the buried garden.
Hans is dead,
the daughters scattered,
the shingled house torn down;
And Alice, where are you?

The Dog Kubla Dreams My Life

I acquired you, old companion,
on impulse from the Palo Alto pound
to satisfy an adolescent
urge for someone all my own.

You crouched shivering on the back
seat of my black '48 Chevy, shedding
fair hair, your obsidian toe-
nails slipping on slick upholstery.

Transported into the redwoods
you tore off down the old highway,
a gold whipcord,
lured back with a bit of steak.

In the cabin bathroom, your corner
stake-out made ferny wastes our outdoor
toilet, as you snarled comic guarding
your own ceramic reservoir.

Tamed with coos and coaxings
into a loyalty hard-won,
I called you *Kubla*
after that nervy invader.

In an attic in Berkeley, you shredded
the socks of my first lover, pawed
ravelled strands beside my rumpled bed,
then patrolled the narrow stairs.

Pacing the pine floor-boards, those wolfish
toes tip-tapped a sentry song. Nobody's guide
dog, you wore no harness, roamed at will.
You could be gone for days prowling

lanes and harbour wastelands or snoozing
contented in some student's kitchen.
They called *Kubla* on Telegraph Avenue,
you glinted sidelong.

When I moved to L. A. I entrusted you to a friend
until I settled in where dogs were welcome.
He said you got lost, wandered off, followed
some family back up to the redwoods.

He claimed I had made you too friendly.
Year later I heard you were killed
the week I left,
running towards a woman
calling *Kubla* from the kerb.

The House We Didn't Buy

I

Cretonne
and the noise from the freeway,
a dusty house where others left
scant trace –
encrusted cables
empty cartons
cat's clawmarks on parquet.

Grey nets blew
in the long cool rooms
elegant in their emptiness.
In the neglected bathroom
somebody else's toothbrush.

What could have been our bedroom
looked out on bedrock
haunted by bodies dumped
in decomposing granite,
slain in other parts of the city.

Low-slung bungalow
we left you behind,
left your rosettes of grass
your cactus garden,
grit in the rusting
hinges of your cupboards,
your chrome radiators.

Who is knocking about
the house we didn't buy?

II

I see a tea ceremony of ghosts
in the spare bones of your rooms.
Sturdy pre-war ribs support
walls where nobody wants to live.
Someone built you in the lee of the hill.
Terrace full of snails,
a view of the Bowl
and too much shade.

Where are your sunny casements?
No traveller can return to that
cool afternoon of rippled shadow,
no slippered foot stumble
on those broken steps
hidden under ivy.

no past
no future
no mantle
no hearth
no fire
no sound.

Young and restless,
we moved on,
north, where the Valley floor
pulses with summer.

With One Continuous Breath

I have stepped out
onto that same patch of grass
a thousand times,
it is my Heraclitean stream.
You, jingling your car keys,
me, wearing the low-cut lilac dress,
eager for the Italian meal,
unsure, always unsure.
Only your hieratic gestures;
tipping the head waiter,
calling him by name,
assure me you too are uncertain.

Up on the hill our house
dissolving in a sea of lights,
under chaparral, granite decomposing
our oranges slightly sour,
more lemons than we could ever use,
the jacaranda;
life in such profusion.

Again and again I step
out of the car your father gave us,
too posh
too grand for newly marrieds.
The grass springs sere under my lilac sandals,
petal sleeves, beehive, eyes absurdly kohled.

With one continuous breath
I absorb the pungent night air,
never dreaming
that from all our years together
this moment only will sting.

Upstate New York

The Pie Stand in Upstate New York, 1961

Night sifting over fields and stone walls
tires sponging down the long, springy grass
where dew collects.
Unseen creatures scatter
as our white Rambler inches
toward the glowing shack, where insects
flying in the head beams
carry the light away with them.

We park in the damp field,
the windows are down
warm air envelopes us, redolent
with boysenberries and apples.
Steam rises from the pies aslant the counter,
while our children dance behind us,
their pale arms
flying in arcs;
their faces moons.

Cars circle the shack
slicing the darkness
around the lighted kiosk.
My husband's head is turned away,
he is wondering
who will serve us tonight
under the revolving stars.

Behind the steaming pies
stands a woman in a checkered apron.
She is raising her knife
ready to cut the fresh-baked
discs into wedges,
her arms shine.

Our children are clapping
their hands behind us
crying for ice cream;
and those insects
who stole the light,
were they fireflies?

Living Near a Nuclear War-Head
Storage Base

Kennedy was not yet dead when I lived in Rome,
New York, upstate on the old Iroquois Trail.
The thin rind of road skirting the door enclosed
a clean wedge of pine barrens and surprising
ponds bristling with snapping turtles.

Once the jaws lock over an arm
or a wrist, or a finger, they never relent.
To release the afflicted limb
you must chop off the scarlet neck.

Kennedy was still living the afternoon I walked,
clumsy in my husband's boots
alone through virgin snow sword-slashed with pines,
black web of haunting lines,
staff and notation of an unsung song.

I was sinking in fresh snow up to my knees,
plunging into the crusting afternoon.
Something sighing in the pines gripped my city girl's heart
exalted and all as I was, turned loose in the sun-shot snow.

Terrified, I retracted the day back
through the cold trough I had ploughed coming out,
past the sleek pond's submerged turtles,
secret weapons iced for future reference
when they would haul out on logs and lie
snapping in the sun while berries ripened.

Before the snow melted, our white
Samoyed and black Alsatian puppies
caught the neighbour's Leghorns and tore
them to bits, feathers flying white
on white as we watched in horror
from behind the picture window
the untutored savagery of puppies killing for sport.

Later that Spring, the Samoyed was hit
by a county truck. The road crew threw
her whiteness up on the load of boughs
cut from pines obscuring the road,
the dark road that linked the long houses
where the five Iroquois Nations met.

The ditches were singing the day our landlord
tractored over with his only son.
Playing in the sand, the boy lifted a stone
shielding a nest of grass snakes,
moving whips of green.
Dropping the stone they sheltered under
he smashed them to bits
until they blurred into brokenness.

A few miles down the road the nuclear
war-heads stored at Griffiss hunkered
down under their grass caps, behemoths
never ageing, metal brain boxes ready
to convulse over Cuba.

Buck Mountain

Poems from Buck Mountain

I

On the beach below the cabin
my neighbour digging clams,
arm, spade, hand
one dark scythe.
Making his solitary supper
chowder in a bucket
he splashes in the wine
he does not dare to drink.

II

I have three daughters;
the eldest sleep in the cabin lofts,
the youngest sleeps far away.
My thoughts fly to her
like the tongue to the space
where a tooth has been.
When she comes north
I no longer notice the ruts
criss-crossing our flooded road.

III

Summer picnic in a field
my curving belly
tightens like a tent.
Through a frieze of Queen Anne's lace
the horse barn's soaring roof
bends the horizon,
ghostly floating slates.

IV

My neighbour no longer lives at Buckhorn.
His new house straddles the rocks.
The lodge made his present wife gloomy.
On hot days, cedar resin
smelled like another woman's perfume.
In the deserted garden under the pines,
nettles and morning glories contend for space
where the deer once nibbled his roses.

V

Inside my neighbour's barn
his cast-offs gather dust.
Forks tangle in the rusting beater's tines.
Nesting swallows slice the light
flowing through the open door.
Painted swallows soar on plates
that have known the rat's paw.
I take some to wash in the cabin sink,
deep as a horse's trough.

VI

In the empty loft,
a golden mountain.
Heaps of dead wasps
crunch underfoot.
Outside in the orchard,
living wasps
drown in the warm innards
of apples.

VII

My neighbour's wife works at the fish farm.
She binds her long curls up in a net.
Fluorescent light bouncing
off the iridescent scales,
the smoke and chatter of the other girls
all give her migraine.
For comfort, throughout the Gospel Hour
she holds her husband's hand.

Goodbye to Our Cabin

The latch has not yet rusted
on our cabin door.
This morning when I lifted it
and peeked inside,
expecting dust and spiders,
I found the kettle still
steaming on my iron stove
and cups we had drunk from
years ago draining
in the china sink.

Out on the water, the sun
still tantalizes the North Shore
throwing stray beams
across our mossy roof.

Summer Picnic

Salmon shaped headland
juniper scaled, Lord Eagle
draws his silent snare
above the bay.

Red, soft-fleshed salmon leap
splitting water's crepe, where
minnow millions bubble and spiders
feed on stranded bloat.

Boats head out hopeful,
men cast, hooking
fins of spent hungerless fish,
death arrows snagged on barbless hooks.

Down banks of shell and charcoal
we bathers parade where twisted
roots of madrona expose themselves
as the sea pulls earth's element in.

Under a dome of air our fires
flicker, built of drift above
wet pebbles. Paper plates, cups,
vegetable spawn crumble to clean ash
while the covering tide pulls night's
dark cape around our cove.

Settled Life Makes Me Crazy

Wearing paper slippers
a bathrobe inked 'V. A. HOSP.'
my friend was taken out to a baseball game,
back and forth
back and forth
sewn leather smashed into a wire frame.

Gossip has it he went mad under fire,
he confides years later,
'I lost the desire to live
and never got out of my bunk.'

Foreign shade shelters us
an island of stop-time
far to the north of his diagnosis.
Married to an heiress,
minor league,
he crouches beside his taxi
a gift of the in-laws,
hiding from passengers off the ferry.

Red bandana catches sweat,
his berry eyes conspire,
'We'll go drinking in the woods
till the last ferry leaves –
they'll never find us.'

Branches droop across the letters
'ISLAND TAXI'.
Behind the van, sun dances,
oil films deep Sound water around the pilings,
creosote gives us back the reasons
we both fled the city.

He says, 'Settled life makes me crazy.
It's those paper slippers and the asylum robe.
Can you believe they let me out in such a state?'

Driftwood

My son brought home a pike for me to cook
disdained by the man who snagged it
from Galway's rain-swollen Corrib.
We didn't know the Irish don't eat coarse fish.

When he began to clean it on a stump
in the back-garden of our terraced house
I saw you standing long ago on the beach at Squaw Bay,
your hip-boots shining in the slipping
light of late autumn.

You were holding the last salmon of the season
filleting it neatly on a stump
we rescued from a litter of logs
broken loose from their close flotilla
somewhere in Puget Sound.

No fish ever tasted so sweet
as the ones you cooked
peppered and stuffed with lemon and thyme
over the salty blaze of driftwood.
We burned it in the mammoth cast-iron furnace
downstairs in the basement
where dozens of jars of preserves
stood winking in the wavering light
thrown back up from the bay.

We packed it tightly in the kitchen stove –
the natives said the salt would corrode the grate –
pregnant, I hauled logs for an empire
up from the beach,
while out on Squaw Bay you reef-netted
sockeye and silvers, each streaming in season.

In June, when I went into early labour,
wild roses covered the acres of split-
rail fencing enclosing our farm;
and as we raced to catch the ferry
fourteen herons stood along the shore,
sentinels to our lives.

Ireland

Son

Son,
you've grown too large
for our small semi-detached,
your black suede shoes are as big
as coal buckets,
you'll soon be dancing on
the ceiling like Fred Astaire.
You curl up on the couch
like a flex around a kettle
and if you were to peer up through the chimney,
your brown thatch would sweep
the cobwebs out of the sky.

In the Garden

The way the northwest wind
scythes down our street,
stunts the trees,
feathers leaves that should be fronds,
breaks the mountain ash in shards.
After dark
I tie the branches up with old rope.

Problems stalk the garden
haunting each leaf and twig –
will the dahlia snap
the woodbine smother
the seedlings wither
in their sockets of earth?

Endless cups of coffee
in the haze and wind
pulling weeds
blight's twin
hoping black spot, root rot,
mildew, mould will stay away.

Underneath the asters' frazzled tops
the slugs bite deep
melanotic
seemingly asleep.
Wild pansies wave
fey runaways.

The seeds of leafy rampants
masquerade as plants,
weeds entire.

We never sense the gloom
of gardens running wild
on those billowy days
we spade our paths,
dig beds where rubble lay,
not counting the mild hours
that mark the sun's wide arc.

What made me plot to tame nature,
wily in every fibre,
outsmarting manmade plans?
I kneel in the wet grass
and begin again.

Behind the spokes of an old bicycle
wedged in against the wall
a crow
anomalous in death
all blackness pointing skyward,
a fallen star.

In the Women's Cancer Ward

I – Breakfast

Across from me a Dublin woman
drops her spoon
milk spatters from her porridge,
'I can't use my hand –
soon I won't be able to tie
the ribbons in my daughter's hair.'

The unseen child takes shape,
silky ribbons bobbing
the mother's breast heaves
beneath her bargain pearls.

II – Waiting for Treatment

We're targeted for treatment
red noughts and crosses
quilting our skin.
The young woman who knits
acts unperturbed.
'I'm barely scratched,' she tells us,
'They just removed the lump.
Early stage –
I don't really need radiation.'
Her needles click,
she drops a stitch.

A woman from Donegal says,
'He cut me from the shoulder
to the waist.
Old-style surgeon,
did I jump the gun?
Someone suggested a second opinion.'

She kneads her hands
rolling invisible dough
then stares down at the floor.
No one speaks.

III – *Watching the News*

Wearing her leather money-belt
like a bandolier,
her painful tongue and gums
have betrayed her.
Still the Sergeant Major barks orders:
'Switch the channels.'

She doesn't want news from the Republic,
not even from Ulster.
She colonizes the day room
mounts surveillance on the TV
subjects us all to nasal
static from the BBC.

IV – The Royal Wedding

In the day room
Diana's veil fills the screen,
her smile stretches from London
to Ballymun.
Death watches in a pink jumper,
chain-smoking.

Vows professed,
the straight-backed chairs
empty their tired occupants,
ruined breasts, lost wombs
into the hot July afternoon.

V – The Young Bride

The young bride lies outside her covers
wearing a white blouse.
Buds inside her breasts scatter their seeds
down her spine.
They float in the furrows
of her bones.

On our daily walk she moves
carefully, becoming a shadow
under the flashing canopy of trees.

At the end of the avenue
she asks to turn back, explaining,

'My husband will be here at 4.'
She buys him chocolate from the hospital kiosk,
I link her on the the lawn.

VI – *Blurred Vision*

At tea time I peel an orange
for the woman with the eye patch,
her vision is blurred.
She tells me of her caravan in Clare
where she'll be going for the summer,
of her children
singing in the sand
and a husband who will be her eyes.

The long twilight tints the bedclothes,
her time is short
yet summer stretches on forever.

VII – *Raspberries in Rathgar*

Each evening after treatment
I walk slowly into Rathgar
to buy baskets full of nippled berries.
I can't get enough of them,
their ruby juice runs down my chin.

More that swallows,
raspberries make a summer,
their season so short

so delicious,
shop fronts full of punnets.
Buying raspberries,
I'm running in a race I cannot win.

VIII – *The Night Nurse*

Pushing night's trolley through the pneumatic hush,
back and neck erect,
caryatid with silver braids,
veins twine the pillars of her legs.
3 a.m., cradles the insomniac whispering,
'My dear, sleeping pills don't suit you,
we'll throw them all away.'

Will my blood, scoured with mustard gas,
hermetically blasted by a thousand suns
flow pure again and strong?
And will the weekend
when I see my children
ever come?

I See Lovers

These are the sunlit hours I envied others,
walking in the dry slopes above the cabin,
pine needles slick underfoot,
where someone is painting a meadow,
someone chopping fruit in a tiled kitchen.

I see lovers
framed in an open window,
the same window through which I glimpsed my friend,
mouth like a melon,
pull my husband towards her.

I had stepped out to wash my hands
in a room at the end of a dark hall.
I could hear my sleeping children coughing in their cots;
one's curls were wet,
the other's fontanelle still throbbed.

Outside, archaeologists were unearthing
the skeleton of a young woman.
Inside her delicate cage of ribs,
the bones of her baby arranged themselves
skull down, ready to be born.

On Barna Strand

Hangover weather; the spirit's
fuel evaporates amongst buckets
and babies, thoughts of wrecked
marriages, hidden black attachments.

Beside me a handsome couple
read while their young
sons pitch beach
fires behind small dunes.

Tinted glasses angle down
her patrician nose. His legs,
muscle dark in shorts. Perfect
stripes even the children's shirts.

Tights off, I escape, flat-
footed in the rutted
sand, towards rocks tide-pocketed,
convoluting sea and sky.

Cliffside, an older couple picnic.
His ruddy beard wags
against his sun-burned chest. Her head
tilts skyward, sipping tea.

Brown trousers rolled
the man appears beside me.
We are wading
in water up to our ankles.

Tights on, his companion follows
fretting. Unable to wade,
she falls behind,
out of earshot.

We speak of seals beyond
the children's graveyard, of last
week's schooling dolphin. His ample
voice rumbles above the humming water.

For a moment I imagine
on empty days, and days flashing
brightness, we walk here
often in wrack and wind.

The tide flows in; silt
soaks the rolls of his trousers,
the folds of my skirt. At the last
pool we separate.

Beside my empty blanket, the young
couple still lean against striped back-
rests, while below the broad
proscenium of the beach,
the sea recedes.

Grace

Since she turfed out the drunken coalman
her head is filled with nothing but God;
every bush in her back garden
is burning with voices,
every rock left from the builders' rubble
rolls back to reveal the empty tomb.

She speaks in tongues in the scullery
and polishes the stairs in haste
to get back to her King James Bible
which she quotes with an angelic grace
that belies years of Mills and Boon
and the Sunday Star.

Her child has a problem
the doctors cannot cure
but this only bolsters her faith
that he will be healed
before the new school is finished.

Since she turfed out the drunken coalman
her head is filled with nothing but God;
she walks among rattling coal lorries
rapt in a nimbus of light.

Cairo

Rain straifes our city bus.
Beside me, a lady with tinted glasses remarks
she has no umbrella,
she lost it months ago in Paddington Station,
that cave of bears.
No doubt some station master's daughter
is sporting it through London's seamless streets
or, knowing how they clean the trains,
it lies still furled in a corner of the luggage rack.
She can see it lying there;
(she'd give anything to have it back).

'Oh, I've had other umbrellas,
a green one once with a broken spine
that I couldn't lose in a fit,
but this umbrella was special
because it doubled as a third leg.
I need that, you see, a disguised walking stick
and the handle, a carved bird.

Ah, but one takes one's comforts
in the ordinary little courtesies.
Just today a lovely man gave me a lift
when I asked directions
to a furniture showroom out the road,
'Hop-in', he said and I was young again,
I was twenty and life was full of adventure.

I've bought myself a little house, you see,
and I want to furnish it.
Today was a very lucky day for me,
asking directions,
but nowhere in the world have I met people
who know so little about where they are –
the men are desperate but the women are worse.

Is it because they live under their
husband's protection?
Women do that, you know, they follow money,
they do, you know, they really do.
Myself, I'm a tough old bird, a wanderer, solo.
Did you know the French are building
a tunnel under Cairo?
Must be bread and butter in it.
The women here wouldn't even know
where Egypt is.'

The fierce low sun bulleting in
the scumbled bus
lights up her purple-tinted glasses.
I am hurtling beneath baking city streets;
I see Cairo.

Moby Dick in the Burren

We came upon you
today's central image
whale-shaped monolith
basking in a pond of leafy sunlight
trawling a harpoon of shadow;
all your sailors, your Jonah's
secure
in your rocky innards.

The slow swell of the wind
billowing up the limestone furls
surrounds us in a sea of soft sound.
Centuries pour in waves around us
as we puzzle out your probabilities.

Tensile bones
you sleep so securely
under your cap of rock
where we lounge in the bee-strewn grass
beside you
posing in mock studies against your
immensity,
like tourists in those faded photos
beside the Pyramids.

Here history aspires
to the symmetry of myth
and Melville's mighty symbol

acquires accidental form
beached in the Burren
above the limestone sea,
intact, until flayed open
for secrets that Ahab never found.

Flooded Fields

Mirror of night's phantasms
you lie draining
bloodied by the sun.

Fertile receptive surface
alert at first light
underneath, a seeded life
prolapses.

Womb of air
sheep stare from your margins
unrequited.

Nothing grows there
even lilies cannot root
where drowned poles and trees
protrude.

Your windrift ridges
mimic fertility until
sucked up by the sun
you vanish
becoming a breath of air.

The Mountain Has Always
Been A Holy Place

I – Croagh Patrick Speaks

Before the glacier scoured my skin
I bled green seedlings,
wildflowers fell from my eyes
who now am bristling with gorse.
Being quartzite has its consolations:
I dazzle.

The first god up here
had a cauldron that never emptied
yet he grew bored
(in plenty there is never challenge).
He longed to see himself reflected
in the blasting glaze
of the cauldron's empty innards:
miracles never consoled him.

I was there in the time of Lugh
when the stones were screaming
and when Dagda the Good
cast spells so great
that people perceived not the night
nor felt hunger and thirst.
I saw him turn a beautiful woman
into a pool of water
because they both desired it.

I saw Oisin old with laments
shudder at the sight of Patrick's crozier,
the melancholy Patrick who came and brooded
heavy-hearted for a homeland
he believed he could see from my summit.
He preached to ease his heartache
and drew pilgrims to climb me:
their eyes embers.

They swarm my flanks like insects
until I shrug,
and among the thousands I protect,
one is lost.
The years fly by in the shape of birds
while Druid winds lash
every bush and branch and pulsing atom
in my thorny bones.

II – Death on Croagh Patrick

Clouds hung in the shrouded morning
a warning not to ascend
the dark cone swarming with ghosts.
Out along the coast vigorous hues
dilute the sullen light.

While we ramble through a ruined abbey
seeking out its dank remainders
a child is falling,
the very act a parabola
subscribed over and over
delivering up at the foot of the mountain
this silent disaster,
a crowd huddled bewildered
beside a stone wall
the small body bundled by on a stretcher
wisps of young hair escaping
the blanket's closure.

Time, wind back,
gravity reverse that dying fall.
Would we could enter the ruin
all over again
and come out to nothing,
not this body, still as a doll.

III – A Pilgrim Speaks

'The mystery was the dark,
the dark and the candles of the penitents
glittering like sparks blown from a chimney
snaking up the mountain in a river of light,
and then in the midst of all this,
to look out on the magnificence of Clew Bay
with a clean soul.

           Stations
           confessions
           purges

several priests at the oratory on top –
the penance would be done for the year and then
they would have a good little screw in the car
on the way back.
The serious sinners came down with
holes in their feet, profusely bleeding.

I often wonder how many really believed in St. Patrick,
that he could cure anything.
Or were the old night pilgrimages more like pagan
                              carnivals
when all hell broke loose –
'Up – Bohola, Ballyhaunis, Lisdoonvarna?'
On Reek Sunday they'd come from all over the country,
stopping at their favourite pubs along the way.
In the shebeen closest to the Reek
they might have to wait an hour for a pint,
and then fall up the mountain feeling everybody's
arse if they could get away with it.

69

And a lot of them fell down the mountain too,
into the steams and onto the rocks.
The side of the reek would be littered
with bottles:

> Guinness bottles
> beer bottles
> baby Powers.

The crowds are dwindling now that the
yahooing and tomfoolery are gone,
but it's said they've found gold in the river
that flows down by the Reek.
There will soon be another kind of pilgrimage,
one to the other god.

The mystery was the dark,
the dark and heaven and hell.
Still,
in spite of all the old nonsense,
the hooligans, the bums, the lot,
somebody would experience God.
Everyone who went up the mountain
would come back down with a tale to tell;
each one would have seen the bloody stars.'

IV – Hy Brasil: Summer 1980

An island in Clew Bay
sliced, double-domed
sun-shattered.
Turf-tensed rabbits punctuate
dense mats of grass.

John and Yoko bought
this drumlin
in an icy, wayward bay,
a harbour silted up
to shipping –
his Hy Brasil.

Up on the Holy Mountain
a farmer's wife
suds to the elbow
looks out at the always
empty bi-partite kingdom
sees

under a Mayo sky
John and Yoko nude
picnicking
amongst sturdy tussocks,
thinks
'How like an ark the island looks.'

Hy Brasil: legendary island, visible every seven years.
Anyone who looks upon it will die.

Out There

Out There

*'Scientists confidently predict they will be able to see
right to the edge of the universe using Hubble.'*

'At the round earth's imagined corners'
no angels blow their trumpets
the dead do not arise.
Etherealised, they howl through space
vortexing storms that rage
a thousand years.

In shadow's circumference
black blossoms.
Shadows of shadows posit
other worlds
more chaotic that our own
with its tidy hills and valleys.
New stars are born
trailing clouds of glory
eons long.

None of this mimes history
unless Plato was correct
and out there
a black and perfect world
sucks up each wish, each kiss,
each criminal intent.
Out there
auroras pulsate
with dynamic life
unspent.

At one of the round earth's corners
a panicked, suited father
dashes from his car
arms out, palms up
to stop his two young children
racing headlong towards a bus,
drops to his knees at the kerb
and kisses each one's cheek.

Back buckled in his seat
he bows his head at the wheel
then shifts into reverse;
he has just seen
the edge of the universe.

Schrödinger's Cat

Cat
Schrödinger put you inside a box
forever sealed
concealing your fate.
We will never know until
we look inside the metaphor
if you are in there or not.

Fat, substantial cat
waxing and waning
like the moon in the dark,
rising in some minds
setting in others.
There may be an infinity of cats
in there by now
in as many worlds as minds will manufacture.

Oh wondrous cat, galactic cat,
universes pulsate in the folds of your fur
and your star-crossed fate
purrs in the interior
of your sturdy, experimental box.
Tiny atoms erode under your nose
releasing or not releasing
the lethal gas of proof.

Whether you are dead or alive
you exist, kitten and cat in an instant,
both springing forth and lying still.

Abstract you have substance
you never had in life.
Quotidian feline,
like the sacred cat of the Pharaohs
guarding the hinged lid
of all our dark uncertainties.

On First Seeing the Sea at Seventeen

If matter is frozen light,
what did the Montana boy
first see at seventeen
when light made manifest
broke its dense brilliance at his feet
on the gritty New Jersey shore.

Far from the seared tableland
tilting always towards winter,
far from the singing Arctic winds,
far from the ice shards
stabbing his father's fields
with their buffalo humps
of rusting animals,
far from his mother's silted jars
and her root cellar's blind, sprouting eyes,
to this salty paradise
silvering New Jersey.

He drew its wholeness in,
rocked in a watery cradle
unknown to those born near water.
Reborn, he exhaled his prairie life
as healers fill ordinary tumblers
with myriad ills.

The boy born inland knows his destiny
when he first sees ocean,
and he will not leave it for long –
not to ride the blistering summer mesas
nor to work his father's farm.

He will turn his back on the land
and go towards the plangent booming
orchestra beyond the dunes.

Burial Instructions

I don't want to be cremated,
my clothes sent home in a bag,
my ashes sifted from the furnace grate
for my Claddagh ring
and gold fillings.

No, plant me,
like my Grandmother's blazing dahlias
in the subsuming earth,
where I can be lifted,
where there's a chance of resurrection.

How about the hump-backed hill
beyond Barna
riddled with Celtic crosses,
or the sun-shot meadow on Orcas
facing steaming Mt. Baker.

On second thought
Westwood is best,
beside my mother
where the mocking-bird sang
the night she was buried.

You might know the spot
because that's where they placed
Marilyn's ashes
in a pale marble crypt
looking across at our family plot.

They say it's Joe
provides the perpetual rose,
but no one knows for certain.
Be sure you put me in the ground
where I will have a chance to rise.